KU-515-123

ROSS AND CROMARTY

A pictorial souvenir

NESS PUBLISHING

2 A Ross-shire panorama from Culbokie on the Black Isle looking west towards Maryburgh and Dingwall

ROSS AND CROMARTY

From the Black Isle to Kyle of Lochalsh

Welcome to Ross and Cromarty!

The old county of Ross and Cromarty stretches across northern Scotland from the town of Cromarty at the eastern tip of the Black Isle to Kyle of Lochalsh on the western coast. Between these extremes lies an area similar in size to that of Cyprus, in which can be found a range of scenery and settlements not easily bettered by any other Scottish county. The charm of historic towns like Cromarty (opp.) is complemented by the awe-inspiring grandeur of mountains such as those of Inverpolly and Torridon.

As the name suggests, Ross and Cromarty was formed by the amalgamation of two counties in 1889. Although smaller, the county of Cromarty-shire was the senior partner, originating in the 13th century. The amalgamation made more sense than some such arrangements because Cromarty comprised a number of pockets of territory dotted around Ross-shire, so that the two administrations were already well mixed in with each other. Today, Ross and Cromarty is part of the Highland Region, but its name continues to be much in evidence even if its boundaries are no longer so clearly defined.

Ross and Cromarty has been home to its share of notable people. Maelrubha (642-722) founded the church in Applecross in 673 (see p.65) and was regarded as the patron saint of that part

Looking down to Cromarty and the Cromarty Firth from South Sutor

6 A view of Kyle of Lochalsh from the approach to the Skye Bridge

of Scotland. Hugh Miller (1802-1856) is perhaps the greatest alumnus of more modern times to come from the region. The Cromarty birthplace of this remarkable geologist, writer and church leader is open to visitors (see p.10).

This book takes readers on a tour of the county that starts in the east on the Black Isle, goes around the Cromarty firth to Tain, then strikes north-west to Inverpolly. It then tracks roughly south-west through a variety of coastal and inland locations such as Ullapool, Kinlochewe and Loch Carron before reaching the southernmost extremity of the county around Kintail.

This exploration shows the great variety that sums up Ross and Cromarty. Whether it's palm trees in Plockton, oil rigs in Nigg Bay, fishing ports like Ullapool, inland seas like Loch Maree, red squirrels or golden eagles, each one makes its special contribution to this wonderful slice of Scotland.

Liathach towers above the village of Torridon

8 The spit of land that is Chanonry Point stretches out into the Moray Firth from the south side of the Black Isle

10 Hugh Miller's cottage with the Miller House beyond

Cromarty Courthouse, built 1770-1773

Cromarty Lighthouse

12 The village of Rosemarkie, on the southern coast of the Black Isle, seen from Chanonry Point

Groam House Museum in Rosemarkie is dedicated to presenting and interpreting Pictish culture. Displays are focused on 15 Pictish carved stones

14 The ancient town of Fortrose lies just to the west of Rosemarkie. These attractive buildings are in the town centre near the cathedral remains

Fortrose Cathedral was built in the first half of the 13th century. What remains today is only a small part of its original size

16 Chanonry Point lighthouse. The name is derived from the nearby 'chanonry' cathedral at Fortrose

Chanonry Point is also a good place to see the Moray Firth dolphins

18 A few miles west of Fortrose the village of Munlochy is situated at the head of this beautiful bay

North Kessock, just across the water from Inverness, gives tantalising views down the Beauly Firth to the distant mountains beyond

20 The Town Hall and Museum in Dingwall, county town of Ross-shire

The Hector Macdonald Memorial, Dingwall

Dingwall is where the railway lines to the far north and Kyle of Lochalsh diverge. The plaque recalls First World War activity

22 The railway lines may be long gone but the spa town of Strathpeffer has preserved its attractive Victorian station, which is home to the Highland Museum of Childhood

Strathpeffer Pavilion, opened in 1881, is a busy venue for the performing arts, weddings and conferences

24 Ben Wyvis, 1045 metres, dominates the area north of Strathpeffer and Dingwall and is seen here at sunrise

26 A general view of Strathpeffer, an excellent base from which to explore Easter Ross

Castle Leod, just outside Strathpeffer. It has been home to the same family for 500 years. It is open to the public on selected days each year – see back of book for contact information

28 Tain Collegiate Church, built between about 1370 and 1460 to house the shrine of St Duthac, an early medieval saint who was born in Tain

A panel in Tain's Pilgrimage Centre which illustrates and describes one of the miracles credited to St Duthac

 Tain Tolbooth, built between 1706 and 1733

Detail of the Nigg Stone, an important example of a Pictish carving. It is housed in Nigg Old Church (a few miles south of Tain) and is part of the Highland Pictish Trail which runs through eastern Ross & Cromarty. The Trail continues north-east to Tarbat

A life-size bronze of Pictish Queen at Tarba

Tarbat Discovery Centre is a museum situated in an old church in the coastal village of Portmahomack. It is next to the site of the only Pictish monastery found in Scotland

32 Portmahomack is situated a few miles east of Tain on the Tarbat Peninsula. An idyllic location with views across the Dornoch Firth to Sutherland

The harbour. Portmahomack's origins date back to the arrival of St Colmac, who established a priory in AD 975

34 Now we move on to the northernmost part of Ross & Cromarty, the wilderness of Inverpolly. Its mos dramatic mountain is Stac Pollaidh (612 metres), seen from the north (left) and the west in close-up

For those who climb it, superb vistas like this await them. Cul Mor (849 metres) is in the distance

36 Overlooked by the mountains of Inverpolly, the Hydroponicum at Achiltibuie has been established for over 20 years and is now *the* centre for the demonstration of soil-less growing in the UK

The ferry 'Isle of Lewis' arrives at the port of Ullapool from Stornoway in the Outer Hebrides

38 Ullapool is located on Loch Broom, south of Inverpolly. It was first laid out in 1788 by the British Fisheries Society and is still a fishing port

A closer view of Ullapool seafront. See also the back cover of this book

40 Loch Fannich is situated in the mountainous heart of Ross & Cromarty, a few miles north of the stretch of the A832 between Achanalt and Achnasheen

42 Looking south along Loch Broom soon after dawn. A salmon farm can be seen in the loch on the left of the picture

Travelling west from Loch Broom brings travellers to more mountainous country. The jagged ridge of An Teallach reaches a height of 1062 metres

44 Continuing westwards: the foaming waters of the Little Gruinard River drain Fionn Loch and meet the sea at Gruinard Bay

The glorious sands and wide-open space of Little Gruinard beach

46 The name 'Gruinard' means shallow fjord or fjord of green water, which this picture bears out. For some places, 'idyllic' doesn't really cover it…

Now looking to the left of the previous view, out across Gruinard Bay eastwards
to the distant mountains of Inverpolly

48 Next stop along the west coast of Ross & Cromarty is Aultbea. Looking across the harbour provides a first glimpse of the Torridon skyline away to the south

Looking north now, across Loch Ewe with the Isle of Ewe on the left and Aultbea in the centre of the picture

50 Inverewe Garden. One of the world's great gardens, Inverewe sprang from the vision and determination of Osgood Mackenzie. It is a National Trust for Scotland property

Inverewe was founded in 1862. This is the walled garden

52 Loch Gairloch is a few miles west of Inverewe. Around its shores are villages such as Gairloch and, pictured here, Smithstown

From Smithstown the northernmost Torridon peaks come into closer view

54 Continuing south-east from Gairloch brings us to Loch Maree. This is one of the great Scottish lochs, 12 miles long and up to two miles wide. Beinn Airidh Charr rises beyond

Further south along Loch Maree, mighty Slioch (981 metres) towers above the water

56 Classic Wester Ross landscape with the length of Loch Maree stretching away on the right

58 At Kinlochewe, just beyond the southern end of Loch Maree.
The Torridon mountains are to the west of Kinlochewe

Contrast in one mountain: on the left, Beinn Eighe's capping of quartzite gives it the whitish colour. Further along the ridge (right) something far more rugged is encountered

60 Liathach, 'the grey one', looks unusually benign. This 1,053-metre peak is not for the faint-hearted. The Torridonian sandstone was formed around 800 million years ago

Winter in Torridon. Tom na Gruagach (one of the Beinn Alligin peaks) is reflected in Upper Loch Torridon

62 Beinn Damph (902 metres) is on the south side of Upper Loch Torridon. This view is from the summit, looking east towards Maol Chean Dearg

In the opposite direction from the same point are Loch Damph and, in the far distance, the Isle of Skye

64 The village of Shieldaig was established in 1800, its name being derived from the Norse for 'herring bay'. Inset: Golden Eagles inhabit the area

The Applecross peninsula is situated between Torridon and the sea. This is where Maelrubha (see p.4) settled: in the distance on the far side of Applecross bay is where he built his church

66 A quiet autumn day at Kishorn, between Applecross and Lochcarron.
Inset: Pine Martens might be seen in Wester Ross

Dawn lights up the village of Lochcarron. We are now south of Torridon and east of Applecross

68 A few miles inland from Loch Carron, in Strathcarron, is Loch Dughaill, calmly mirroring the surrounding hills

Duncraig is on the south side of Loch Carron, seen here silhouetted in early morning light from Plockton

70 Plockton is one of the most picturesque villages on the west coast of Ross & Cromarty. Its sheltered location and the influence of the Gulf Stream allow palm trees to grow

A Plockton panorama. The village goes back to 1801, this being the year in which plans for a settlement were drawn up

72 Evening light on the Torridon mountains

74 Otters are quite common on the shores of Wester Ross

Eilean Donan Castle is on Loch Duich about seven miles east of Kyle of Lochalsh (see p.6). The present-day castle was rebuilt from 1912 to 1932

76 In the south-western corner of Ross & Cromarty, near Glenelg, are two remarkable survivors of Iron Age architecture: Dun Telve (above) and Dun Troddan (right) Brochs

These strongholds stand about 10 metres high and incorporate a cavity-wall structure as can be seen above. They may originally have been roofed

78 The Falls of Glomach, Kintail, are one of Scotland's highest and most dramatic waterfalls at approx. 115 metres/370ft. A long walk, but well worth it!

One of Scotland's best-loved mountain views, the Five Sisters of Kintail. Fading winter light brings down the curtain on this tour of Ross & Cromarty

Published 2008 by Ness Publishing, 47 Academy Street, Elgin, Moray, IV30 1LR
Phone/fax 01343 549663 www.nesspublishing.co.uk

ISBN 978-1-906549-03-9

Front cover: Torridon mountains in spring; p.1: red squirrel; p.4: detail of Hugh Miller Institute in Cromarty; this page: detail from Dingwall War Memorial; back cover: beware of low-flying ships! Ullapool

Websites and phone numbers (where available) in the order they appear in this book:

www.visithighlands.com
Train services: www.firstgroup.com/scotrail
Friends of the Kyle Line: www.kylerailway.co.uk (T) 01599 534824
Kyle of Lochalsh: www.lochalsh.co.uk
The Black Isle: www.black-isle.info
Cromarty Courthouse: www.cromarty-courthouse.org.uk (T) 01381 600418
Hugh Miller Cottage and Museum: www.nts.org.uk (T) 0844 4932158
Groam House Museum: www.groamhouse.org.uk (T) 01381 620961
Fortrose Cathedral: www.historic-scotland.gov.uk (T) 01667 460232
Dingwall: www.dingwallmuseum.co.uk (T) 01349 865366
Highland Museum of Childhood: www.highlandmuseumofchildhood.org.uk (T) 01997 421031
Strathpeffer Pavilion: www.strathpefferpavilion.org.uk (T) 01997 420124
Castle Leod: www.clan-mackenzie.org.uk (T) 01997 421264
Tain Pilgrimage Centre: www.tainmuseum.org.uk (T) 01862 894089
Tarbat Discovery Centre: www.tarbat-discovery.co.uk (T) 01862 871361
Achiltibuie Hydroponicum: www.thehydroponicum.com (T) 01854 622202
Ferries from Ullapool: www.calmac.co.uk (T) 0800 066 5000
Aultbea: www.aultbea.camusnagaul.com
Inverewe Garden: www.nts.org.uk (T) 0844 493 2225
Gairloch: www.gairloch.co.uk
Kinlochewe: www.kinlochewe.com
Torridon: www.nts.org.uk (T) 01445 791221
Torridon mountains: www.torridonmountains.com
Applecross Heritage Centre: www.applecrossheritage.org.uk
Plockton: www.plockton.com